IN QUIETNESS AND TRUST

PSALMS FOR THE LONELY

LYDIA FELIX

BookLeaf Publishing

India | USA | UK

Made with ❤ on the BookLeaf Publishing Platform
www.bookleafpub.in
www.bookleafpub.com

This book is dedicated to all who feel the weight of loneliness and the ache of being alone. May these pages guide you to find peace in the quiet hours with God and provide strength and solace for your aching soul.

Acknowledgements

I extend my heartfelt gratitude to my dear and near ones who have always supported and encouraged my writing. Your appreciation and kind words have been a source of strength, and your testimonies have brought me this far, enabling the publication of this poetry book – my very first.

I also want to acknowledge the moments of loneliness and longing, the dark hours I had to face and the setbacks and regrets of my life. These experiences, though difficult, were divinely orchestrated for my good. They shaped the words in this book and deepened my trust in God's purpose for my life.

Above all, my greatest acknowledgement goes to God. He has been my guide, my comfort and my strength through every season. Without Him, this journey would not have been possible.

Preface

These poems were born out of the solitary hours, seeking comfort but finding none – except in God. Many have faced moments like these, just as I have. But it didn't end there. These pages tell the story of how I battled through those times and how being in the quietness was far from easy.

Believe me, these psalms of poetry will guide you to find trust in your lonely hours. In this broken world, let us not allow loneliness to overtake us or break us down. Instead, let us learn to be still and trust in the Supreme One, who alone can provide infinite strength to help us overcome.

Loneliness is a Gift

Longing and loneliness are a gift
Not everyone will have it,
Even if they do, not most of the time.

Esteem yourself high being in the solitary,
You will be you, and you will have the power
to know who made you.

You will have an encounter with the High, the
Most High.
Oh, what a privilege that not many will long
to come nigh.

Your thoughts will become strong,
They will show how true you are.

Your best companion it will become,
With the conversation deep and long.
And the Creator of you will join along to
know what you have blamed about.

With a broken heart, you fight,
Asking the Saviour to make you light.
He keeps watching you to show His delight,
Thinking, 'What petition will my child send
me?'

Oh, sleepless nights,
Lonely and fragile.

Finally, she sleeps with tear-dried eyes,
Hoping one day her sorrow will fade,
And thanking the Most High that she
overcame tonight.

Thinking how tomorrow will arise,
Leaving it anyway into the hands of the
Divine.

She dreams hope,
Hope all night!

Your Weakness Can Be Counted

Yes, it can be.

Don't you know that there is grace?
There is blessing?

No fool can comprehend what the heavens
are saying,
But you can, if you want to!

You can boast and be sure of your infirmities.
Never shy, never hide.
Your weakness will speak more than your
strength.

God's power will be made so perfect in you
Than you ever think or imagine it could be.

It will not be granted to many,
But it will be granted to all who rely on Him
at any.
Embrace your loneliness, embrace your
weakness,
For it is a perfect sacrifice for a perfect
Saviour.

Don't you know He dwells so near
Among the broken and trashed,
The weak and crushed?

Oh, come with all you have – little or small,
Nothing at all, or words not worthy of all.

He is there for you, oh weak vessel.
He is there to make you the strongest of all.

Gideon said, 'He is tiny of all,'
But God said, 'You are mightier than all.'

Take this message in your quiet time,
And trust Him more in your desert life.

Treasured in Heart

Treasure your thoughts in your heart,
Let it be between you and God.

Let your quiet hours be fruitful and beautiful,
Fulfilling every dream in quietness and
silence.
Think it over; ponder them on.

Release any hard feelings, and let forgiveness
be put on.
Give what you worry about to God, and lay
down what you fear.
Let your anxious thoughts be vaporised
In quietness and hope.

Let your bitter emotions come down.
Share it with God when you bow down.

Surrender completely what you fear and
doubt,
And ask God to take control over what you
wish and aspire.

Commit everything in silence.
Look upon Him in reverence.
You are favoured and blessed.
Never forget to remember that you are
treasured.

Believe He will do mighty things for you
When you surrender in faith and believe He
will do with His might!

Treasure these in your heart.
Treasure these until your prayers come to
pass!
Treasure these
Treasure these in your heart!

Surrender in Silence

Surrender to the Holy One above in silence,
Every want, every need, with complete
reliance.

Every struggle, every pain you bear,
Speak to Him freely; He's always there.

Pour it out like a flowing fountain,
Feel your heart lighten and your strength
retain.

Seek His face, and you'll find His grace,
When you surrender, He takes your place.

Submit to God in quiet adoration,
And expect rewards beyond explanation.

Your tears are not shed in vain,
He sees your hurt and feels your pain.

His ears are never deaf to your cry,
When your plea ascends to His throne on
high.

Surrender, even when words do not come,
Let your silence speak more when your heart
feels numb.

Doubt not once your prayer is made,
For remember, even your sighs bring His aid.

Help is near; help is on its way,
When you surrender to Him every day.

As you've learned to bow and pray,
In silence and worship, His Glory will stay.

You'll see God move in your darkest despair,
when you surrender your heart, which is
beyond repair!

No more

There will be no more weeping,
No more tears to dry.
No more sorrow lingering,
No more trials to make you cry.

It is done.
It is finished.

God has heard your plea;
Wait for His decree.
He will come to comfort you,
But wait in stillness for His dew.

You were indeed wounded and torn,
And it's true He left you forlorn.
But trust – He will mend every pain,
Healing you whole, with no scars to remain.

Don't you know He is the Just King?
Soon, His justice will brightly spring.
Because His love is deep and true,
His grace will surely bloom for you.

Blessed are they who patiently wait;
They will never be ashamed or faint.
His face will shine like morning dew,
And He will wipe your tears anew.

Trust Him more when it's hard to believe;
His promises are true and will never deceive.
His love is steadfast, unchanging and pure;
In His hands, your victory is sure.

It is done.
It is finished.

Believe – you will cry no more.
Relief and comfort are at your door.
Close your eyes and trust each day,
Knowing He's with you in every way.

No more sorrow, no more fear,
No more weeping – God is near.

Suffering is Glorious

Suffering is a hard word,
A pain so deep, often untold.

Suffering for God is an unimaginable
experience,
A test of faith, a journey of trust in pain.

Suffering is worth it; this truth is clear,
When it's for God, it must be sincere.

The crown awaits for sure,
Only for those who endure to become pure.

God is certainly aware that you suffer for
Him,
And He waits to reward you when you meet
Him.

For you must know He will give you glory
instead of shame,
A reward eternal, far beyond fame.

It is hard to breathe,
It is hard to accept this fact of grief.

But worth far more than million-dollar
thrones,
When you learn the worth of a perfect crown
and priceless home.

Be prepared in and off seasons,
To face trials for all His reasons.

Expected and unexpected moments will
come,
To suffer for the glorious one.

Who made you for His good work,
Till He comes back and calls you home

Waiting

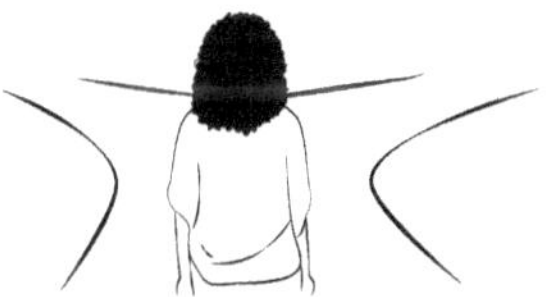

Waiting brings our spirits low,
Making us weak and moving slow.

Our voices sound an absent tone,
Emotions harden, like lifeless stone.

Your groaning hits the heavens from below,
Longing for help to swiftly show.

Asking for strength to stand and walk,
Or at least the breath to speak and talk.

Hoping for a time to shine,
When joy and gladness come to dine.

Lift your eyes to the heavens so high,
Let your heart rest on Him who sees from the
sky.

For relief to come and help so swift,
To grant you rest, a gracious gift.

Leave every burden on God who knows,
Your limits far more than anyone shows.

When tears fall countless, an endless store,
Know they're valued in heaven all the more.

More precious than silver, more than gold,
These tears will answer, a story told.

One day they'll bring you hope and glory,
A blessed end to your heartfelt story.

Leave it to God

Don't shout, don't exaggerate,
Leave it to God and exalt His Name.
He knows what He is doing,
He knows what is right, and He is never
failing.

Never fight with Him,
Instead, do what seems right to Him.
Never bargain, never blame,
He is always faithful and won't leave you in
shame.

Stay in quietness and wait,
He will rescue you and shower His rain.
Not for your gain but for His glory and fame,
He does all things to magnify His Name.

Just hold on for a little while,
Things will unfold with a radiant smile.
You will see and glorify God with praise,
Thanking Him, for He is mighty and great
always.
Stay calm, stay strong,
Leave everything to the Lord where you
belong.
Hope in God; He knows your heart.
Stay calm, stay strong,
Let everything be controlled by the Lord.
Hope in God; He knows your heart.
Leave it to God!

Dreams

When life feels so blue and cold,
Not sure where your faith holds.
Hoping for nothing great, just happiness to
unfold,
Yet knowing life often leaves some dark holes.

Stay calm, trust the process of pain;
Your day will come with colours of rain.
Then you'll shout with joy and say,
'Everything will be alright someday'.

Dream high still, so you can live there,
When hope seems lost and life feels unfair.
Trust only God, for He truly cares,
When your life's dreams turn to nightmares.

Hold on to Him; give your dreams to His
hand,
He'll fulfil them beyond what you've planned.
Be careful for nothing but push through in
prayer,
Trust in His plans, perfect and rare.

He'll add colours to your dreams, gold to your
grey,
Plant vineyards in deserts, make blooms on
the way.
He'll beautify ashes, and you'll come forth as
gold;
Give your dreams to Him – He'll make them
bold.

Rejection

When you feel rejected or thrown,
Don't worry – you're valued and known.
By the One who made you, you are His own;
Why worry when you're treasured like a
precious stone?

Sometimes God separates people from you,
And makes you feel lonely too.
But it's all for a reason, to make you unique
and bold;
You're not less than them – you're different
and more, a treasure to behold.

When your values are being rejected,
When your thoughts are left unconnected,
Write them on your heart's stone,
And treasure them, just as Mary had shown.

They will surely speak one day,
The ones who rejected you will come and say:
'You are pure, glorious and true;
What made you beautiful and so renewed?'

You will smile and softly say nothing,
To those who once unvalued your offering.
For the One who made you will give words to convey,
That you're His beloved, treasured in every way.

Mercy

God will show mercy
Mercy to whom He pleases,
You will receive one for you,
If you trust, He is for you.

No one can stand against you,
If you know God's mercy is upon you.
He hardens the heart of Pharaoh,
And provides you His mercy and hope for
tomorrow.

If you follow His mercy, you will find life–
Life in fullness, without compromise.

If you follow mercy, you will be righteous,
And your good works will be seen as obvious.

If you follow mercy, you can find honour.
It will be on its way, sooner.

Be honest and show yourself as you are,
without reluctance;
He will surely show His mercy in abundance.

He is very generous in giving it to you;
Receive it and be cautious to use it as if it's
new.

It can show favour and help you each day,
Helping you cross one day and face the new
day.

His mercy, His mercy–
Seek it and find strength in every way!

Something New

Your expectations will be fulfilled someday,
When you give yourself to the One who made
you, one day.

He will make something new,
Removing what is old and not true.

Just trust His timing–
He will make all things so new.

Your old will pass,
All the suffering and the loss.

The desires of your heart will be fulfilled,
When you surrender to His absolute will.

Something new will surely come your way;
Just hold on and give to God your way.

Commit your ways to the Maker;
He will make your paths straight, and they
will not falter.

The new beginnings will have an amazing
way,
When your life is fully trusted to Him,
To give you a smile and a beautified ray.

There will always be something new–
Something new for those who trust Him fully
and true.

He is a God of new,
Making old things pass and flew.

He wants to make you new,
And remove the old in you.

Trust this mystery of making all things new,
And you will surely smile and thank Him,
For God is good and true!

Let go

Let go of things that worry you,
Leave it to the One who carries you.

He can take it upon His shoulder,
And relieve your heavy burden as you grow
older.

God's yoke is light,
And He wants to give you His might.

Let go of every worry that weighs you down;
Leave it to God in heaven's town.

God wants to make you feel light,
And does not want you to carry this world's
weight.

Relax and let go of every anger and
frustration;
Let God deal with it – come to realisation.

You are not a piece to be thrown out,
But a masterpiece, precious throughout.

Let go of every fear;
You deserve His love and affection very near

You can overcome with God's strength;
Let go of every worry and your ill health.

Let go of the temper that throws tantrums in
life;
Let in His peace, freedom from strife.

Let go, let go and let heaven heal you more;
Let go, let go and let your soul renew and
soar!

Let go, let go!

Worthy

You are worthy beyond compare,
Even when others treat you unfair.
You are valued and cherished,
Even when others wish your life to perish.

The world will never understand coal's worth,
Until it transforms into diamond through its
rebirth.
There's a time and a process to be adorned,
For every soul that feels forlorn.

Your worth is not measured by people's views.
Nor by the recognition of what you do.
It lies in the gaze of the One who made you,
Who sees your heart, pure and true.

When you feel unworthy,
Remember, you're adorned with beauty.
Your recognition lies with the Maker,
Not with the doubter or the traitor.

The world will never know a pearl's delight,
Until it's washed ashore, glowing bright.
There's a time and process for you to rise,
And be praised more, beyond the skies.

God has a time to lift you high;
Until then, stay still and quiet; don't sigh.
One day, all eyes will see the wonder in you,
And proclaim aloud, 'You're worthy and true.'

Now the world will know the value of you,
And regret the friendship they once
withdrew.
They'll long for the lost days that never
return,
To cherish the essence of the friend they
spurned.

Still Hoping?

Where is your hope right now?
Where does it lie in your row?
Do you still hope–
Hope for good things to come?

Keep hoping till there is sunshine,
Your darkness will leave you sometime.
There will be a clear sky,
When your eyes have run tear-dry.

Hope when your life feels tired,
When nothing's left to be inspired.
When sickness overtakes your pride,
Leaving you dull and dark-eyed.

Does your heart know someone deep,
Who can mend it when you weep?
Who can rent your sorrows for a week,
And repair them to make you feel neat?

My heart says yes – it's Him who knows it well,
The One above who listens when you're unwell.
He gives you hope and a future too,
When your heart feels stuck like a chicken in a stew.

Just close your eyes and pray like a hopeless child,
Who gives a lifetime try to the One so mild–
The One who made this universe so grand,
And holds your life in His mighty hand.

He wants to give you hope and life,
To colour your world with rainbows so bright.
Wonderful things in an amazing way,
More marvellous and beautiful, someday.

Hope and hope,
Never lose faith; let it be strong and roped.
Hope and hope,
Let your heart be firm, like a three-corded
rope.

Hope and hope!
Hope and hope!

Rise from the Ashes

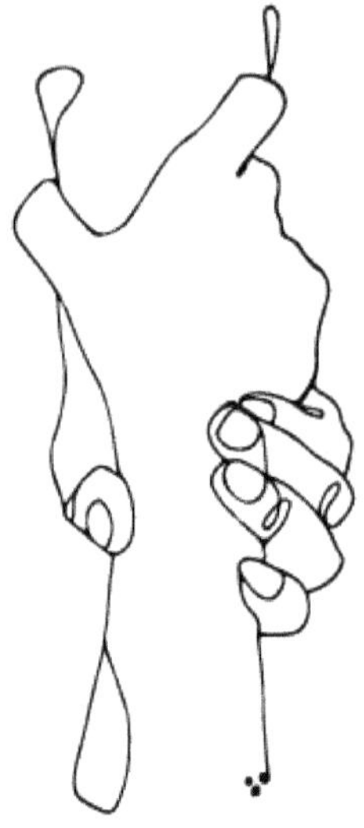

Arise and shine, there is still hope and blessings.
It's enough of being oppressed and shrinking.
Look up – there is hope kept alive.
Arise and walk; God is ready to give you life.

The old story has gone,
The new has begun and is done.
Keep smiling in your pain,
Hoping good will happen again.

Rise from the dusty road,
Heavens will open new doors.
All your heartbreaks will be gone,
You will experience new ways from things
gone wrong.

Your heart, once hurt and longed,
Once perverse and hard,
Will see God's transformation from being
wronged.
Arise and shine – you are no more called
flawed.

Let your heart grow strong,
Even more bold and not rot.
Rise up from the negative thoughts,
Let your mind be transformed and
victoriously fought.

You will turn back and thank for the ashes,
Which made you strong, granting your
wishes.
Newer you have become,
After rising from the ashes, you come!

Seekest Whom?

Whom wilt thou seek when thy heart aches?
When thy heart breaks?
When thy life shakes?
And when thy soul hatred makes?

Seekest whom?
Seekest whom?
Apart from the Lord of heaven and earth,
Who else can satisfy thy heart's true need?

Hast thou found hope?
Hast thou found peace?
What gain hath come from those thou didst
please?
Tell me now – hath thy heart grown whole,
Or bitter still, with burdens on thy soul?

Without God, all thou shalt seek is vain,
Idols bring no joy but deepen thy pain.
Trust Him alone; let thy heart not stray,
Or sorrow shall linger and not fade away.

Leave idols behind, seek God as thine own,
And His mercy and love shall be shown.
The result will be glorious and more,
When thy heart seeks the One who made thee
whole.

Thy desert life shall bear fruits divine,
With streams of honey and milk as a sign.
Pillars of cloud by day and fire by night,
Shall guide thee always, in His glorious might.

Seek Him, the One who is with thee all day,
And He shall never let thee lose thy way.

God Stills

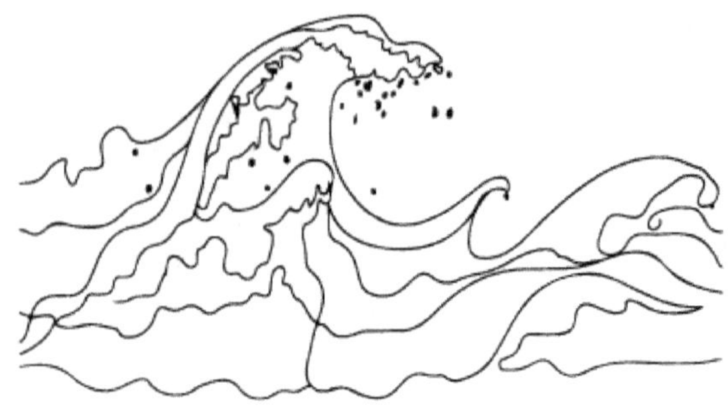

God wants to still your raging soul,
To calm and make your hurting heart whole.
He looks at your scars and softly says, 'Peace,'
With His authority, your fears will cease.

Be still, for all is under His control.
Be still, for peace will fill your soul.
Be still, for His love will never depart.
Be still, for He shields your tender heart.

The storms in your life will surely cease,
At His command, they'll bow in peace.
He rules the waves; they obey His will,
At His voice, the chaos grows still.

There will be peace, this much is true,
For He sees your tears and cares for you.
He'll guide your boat to a safe, calm shore,
And your troubled heart will rage no more.

Trust that He is ruler and King of all,
At His voice, healing answers your call.
With Him in your boat, you'll sail secure,
No harm shall come; His presence ensures.

Be still, and know that He is God,
For He is Exalted above the earth.
Among the nations, His name will reign,
Forever He'll rule, with peace to sustain.

Trust

Trust the Maker who knows you well,
Not the world or fears that dwell.
There will be peace when Him you trust,
For He ordains each step that's just.

Commit your ways unto the Lord,
Both big and small, in one accord.
He knows your heart, your deepest part,
For He's the Maker of every heart.

Delight in Him through night and day,
When storms arise and hearts dismay.
Give Him your pain, your worry, your care,
Cast it on Him – He'll always be there.

Leave it to Him with trust so sure,
His care and love forever endure.
He is God, supreme and great,
Ruler of all and makes your destiny Great

When you trust Him completely and whole,
He'll beautify your broken soul.
Your burdens lifted, your heart made new,
His grace will carry and strengthen you.

Let your trust be in God alone,
Not in men whose promises are prone.
For men will falter, fade and stray,
But God's truth stands forever and stays.

He is the Rock, the foundation eternal,
Unchanging, steadfast and supernal.
So trust the One who never shifts,
And find in Him your greatest gifts.

Desperation

In desperation, I wait,
For someone to comfort when my heart does
faint.
Seeking happiness,
And a warm embrace in times of sadness.

Who will listen to me when I cry,
Till my words stop and my soul is ready to
die?
This desperate longing for love–
No man can ever satisfy.

True love never fails,
It is only God who will help you sail.
Never let your heart dwell in desperation,
For it will lead you to failure in your
aspiration.

Let your desperation rest on God instead,
Rather than on people, leaving you broken
and fed.
In your longing and lonely hours,
Let your desperation be suppressed, not
overpower.

Let it not overtake you,
Take your life, or mock you.
Be bold and strong,
Remember where you belong.

You are not a doormat,
To be in desperation for another's habitat.
You are God's creation, cherished and adored,
Not meant to live in want or desperation's
chord.

Anger

You know it's not good to be angry,
To shout and to let your nerves out.
To get relieved of the pain and the pressure
you hold.

I know it's hard to hold your emotions,
Especially when you don't have anyone to
share your frustrations.

Becoming calm is definitely a difficult job,
But hold on – you will never regret it long.

Anger may help you feel relieved at that
moment,
But it will hurt you so deep, like a sad sonnet.

When there comes a chance for anger,
Just breathe deep and give it to God, for it is
a wise manner.

Lose yourself to God to make Him take
control over you completely

And give it to Him so that He will do the
battle gently

Remember, anger always brings sickness and
sadness.
When you learn to remain calm,
You'll understand the real power of a wise
man.

Keep anger away and give God His way,
You will surely change one day,
And be transformed someday.

Your transformation is for His glory,
You will testify and be merry.

Redeeming Love

Redeeming love, I know,
For it is so pure, like gold.
Yes, it's strong and never cold,
To accept someone like God,
And embrace the stories untold.

Redeeming love will love more,
Unconditional, steadfast and sure.
It carries burdens, heavy and deep,
And prays to the Lord for souls to keep.

Redeeming love, I know,
Can change even the worst sinner I know.
A heart like God's, if you have, you will know,
It's not easy, but His love sets us free, and you
will see.

Redeeming love will not think evil,
For only goodness guides its way.
It lifts, it heals, it understands,
And sees the best in man each day.

Redeeming love, I know,
I long to live in its embrace–
To forgive, to give, to love so true,
Unselfish, pure and full of grace.

Good Things

Good things will happen,
When you have a good God with you.
He is a good Father who never intends evil,
When you trust that He is for your good will.

The good and perfect gift is from above,
It is given to you because He loves you in
abundance.
You will lack no good thing,
When you know your Father has given you
everything.

God will never allow evil forces in your life,
Only good things and blessings to help you
thrive.
Just trust Him, just good things–
Even if evil surpasses, His grace will reign,
and they shall not prevail.

Even the lions will go hungry,
But if you love God and wait patiently,
Your life will never fall into misery.
He is a good Father,
Who gives good gifts, now and forever after.

Oh, how good He is!
Is there anyone who could oppose this?
He is a perfect Father,
With good and perfect gifts for His children,
now and ever after!

Worry Less

Worry less and pray more
It's simple to say but difficult to pray
It has more power than you worry
Instead, pray and be merry
God will do wonders
When you pray and give Him your worries
which are umpty in numbers
Never let your worries stress you
Count them as unwanted for you
God is greater than your worries
And He is ready to answer all your
unanswered queries
Worry less and pray more
This will make life simple and not torn

Worrying will cost you nothing
Even to make you inch better in size or
something
You definitely do not know what holds
tomorrow
But you can trust and place your worries to
the maker, who knows your every sorrow.
Worry less and pray more
Remember to take rest and quieten your soul
Worry less and pray more

Discouragement

When discouragement hits you hard,
Leave it to the One who handles it smart.
Stop dwelling on discouraging words
Instead, focus on what God wants you to do
more.

You are not less than any human,
So never fret when they treat you uncommon.
Turn discouragement into a tool for growth,
And soar high like an eagle, pursuing God's
oath.

Be humble; don't rage against those who speak ill,
Instead, show them that with God, all things are possible still.
There's no room for disappointment in His plan,
For He will fulfil what no one else can.

A time of upliftment is surely near,
And those who discouraged you will stand in astonished fear.
Now, rise up and move boldly ahead,
For the Lord is with you, and your path is Spirit-led!

Bear with One Another

Moments of loneliness will be tough,
And longing for company will feel like
enough.
Past memories of people's behaviour will be
daunting,
But God's forgiveness will help you love them
dearly,
Forgiving, bearing with them and keeping
them near.

Bearing with others is hard,
But perseverance is all you need
To keep your heart from turning to stone.
When you bear with them, God's blessings
will be shown,
And your pain will vanish like a wave on the
shore.

Clothe yourself with love
It will be an easy tool to bear enough,
Not letting hearts grow cold or too warm,
But shaping them to God's likeness,
So they may love you more.

Never lose hope,
For your prayers can change them still.
Your eyes will witness the fruit they bear,
And you will run out of words and tears–
Deep and overflowing–
Thanking God that you bore them
And never wasted the effort of bearing them
more!

No More Shattered

Your dreams will not be shattered anymore,
When you know that your trust lies in God
more and more.
Stay strong and know He will never lead His
children astray,
And will never give up on them, so stay.

Delight till the Lord shows His favour to you,
Let your heavy heart be light and see what
He'll do.
Have faith and do more for His name,
Be bold, knowing your work for Him won't
be in vain.

You will not be broken anymore,
You will not be shattered anymore.
The broken pieces will be gathered,
There will surely be a story to be honoured.

Those who trust in the Lord will never be
abandoned,
Your faith in Him will never go unrewarded.
You will not be shattered,
No more, no more.

The days will come soon,
No more, no more.
You will not be shattered anymore.

Little Strength

God knows you have little strength,
Or at times, no strength at length,
To survive or even to thrive,
To battle life's struggles and strive.

He knows your heart's cries,
Your every sigh and sad goodbyes.
He sees when you prefer lonely company,
Avoiding the noise of irritating humanity.

Yes, God understands your mood,
And the short anger you try to subdue.
Relax, come on, give it to the Lord,
The little strength you have as your reward.

The energy left to think and sleep,
Even the breath you struggle to keep,
Give it to the Lord; let Him create,
Beauty and a chapter that's truly great.

He Crowns

God wants to crown you,
Crown you like a prince and princess too.
He wants to crown you and adore you,
Do you doubt that He'll crown you?

No wonder, He wants to crown you more,
More than you ever imagined before.
He wants to crown you in righteousness,
For the good deeds and sufferings in
perfectness.

He wants to crown you in loving kindness,
That is His admirable nature in highness.
He wishes to crown you in glory and honour,
Ultimately, He does this out of His own
desire; you should ponder.

Finally, He wants to crown you with tender
mercies,
No one can surpass God in this wonderful
character, so sweet.

Remember

Remember how the Lord led you,
Through parched lands, He carried you through.
In brokenness, He mended your pain,
His faithfulness has always remained.

Recall the past, His goodness so true,
And trust He'll guide you in this wilderness too.
Thank Him for all His faithful ways,
Believe He'll fulfil His promises all your days.

Remember how He fed you with manna,
Taught you to trust Him in life's tough panorama.
He kept His word, His promise He made,
Leading Israel to the land for which they prayed.

He will do the same for you – just trust,
His faithfulness endures; His ways are just.
Remember and know, He'll never fail,
With Him by your side, you will prevail.

Roar

Let your fears now flee away,
Be prepared – roar loud today!
God will lift you, take you higher,
Make you stronger, filled with fire.

Roar like a lion, bold and bright,
Gird your loins, stand firm in might.
You will never slip or fall,
Nor turn away from Him at all.

He holds your tears, so deep, so dear,
More than treasures, crystal clear.
Soar on wings that reach the sky,
Like an eagle, strong and high.

You will never faint or tire,
While others slow, you'll climb up higher.
You have waited – just endure,
Soon He'll come and make you roar!

The time is near; do not despair,
You will rise – no more to fear!

Silence

Silence is always the best medicine for your
soul
Give it a try, and you'll surely rise once more.
Stay quiet – that will heal your hurting soul,
Relax and stay calm even when the earth
shakes and brings a strong whirl.

Even if you speak nothing,
Your Maker knows your heart's thinking.
Won't that be enough for Him to fix what's
upsetting?

Let your words fall down as tears,
It is much valued in God's sight as so dear.

You don't have to try explaining things to
others,
It's of no use except for them to forget and
remember it no more.

Let the words stay within you,
But let them not harm or hurt you.
Let your noble character be built and shown
to others,
Let them know that you have stayed quiet
and achieved, not shuttered.

Let your silence tell them who you are,
And that God was with you – not lonely,
struck down in fear.

Let your silence speak,
Speak louder than your character, which is
weak.

Timing

God's timing is always perfect,
Far beyond your imagination and hard work.
He works all things for good,
To make you shine and lift your mood.
He does great things
For those who wait and trust in Him.
Never hurry,
Rushing will only make things blurry.

Let things unfold in their own time,
They will bear fruit when the moment is
right.
Your plans and dreams – yes, He takes them
to heart,
For He loves you unconditionally, never
apart.

His timing is true,
Trust it blindly and live anew.

One Day

One day will prove how much you're worth,
You might be the smallest among your clan
on earth.
But time will show what they fail to see,
You'll rise beyond what they thought you'd be.

Did they belittle you?
Their judgement was wrong, their view
untrue.
Smile and move forward; don't let it stay,
Hatred and anger – just cast them away.

Calm yourself, let them see,
Your time has not yet come to be.
Just like when the wine ran dry,
God's miracle came – none knew why.

A wonder will happen, and you will do it,
Marvellous in sight, none can refute it.
Those who disrespected, mocked and swayed,
Will lower their gaze, in shame dismayed.

For the words of hurt they once did speak,
Now turn to silence, humble and meek.
Not knowing this day, they'd stand and stare,
Hoping and longing to be right there.

One day will come, just wait and see,
Let not your hope grow dim in thee!

Threatened

Oh, your poor soul,
Are you troubled and worn, feeling out of
control?

Let not your heart be filled with despair,
Worrying if problems will grow and ensnare.

Relax and surrender; give all to the Lord,
The One who made you, your shield and
sword.
No danger shall strike, no fear shall remain,
No evil shall touch you or bring you pain.

No more burdens shall weigh you down,
God has lifted them – wear your crown!
The enemy's power is weak and frail,
A powerless shadow, destined to fail.

Smile at him when he tries to scare,
For he knows not the strength you bear.
Alone, you are never – God stands with you,
Mighty and strong, faithful and true.

Say it boldly, declare and proclaim,
'No earthly power shall withstand His Name!
For within me lies a strength so bright,
A heavenly force that wins every fight'!

Delays

God's delays are not His denials,
He loves you and stays so loyal.
In time, the world will see His hand,
Lifting you up, making you stand.

You'll understand why He took time,
To make your life a fruitful vine.
Not just dust, but bright and new,
A masterpiece in perfect hue.

A smile will come; just wait and see,
The delay was meant for destiny.
God does it for the ones He owns,
His precious children, His very own.

Things will turn supernatural,
For waiting long with faith unshaken.
You'll receive a double fold,
The prize for patience, strong and bold.

It wasn't easy, that is true,
Your strength had failed, yet He pulled through.
Not by your might, but by His power,
He held you firm in every hour.

Your waiting will birth a miracle,
And you'll proclaim it as an oracle!

Bold faith

I'm ready to wait for God's perfect will
I know it will not harm, rather be beautiful
I'm ready to wait for His perfect plans
For I know He is Good and does no wrongs
I'm ready to feel the goodness even when it
takes time
For I know He works all things for good for
He says – you are mine
I'm ready to take this bold step of faith
To wait patiently no matter how many miles
it takes
I'm ready to take this path of uncertainty
For I know there are always amazing things
waiting undoubtedly

Fake

I don't want to live my life in fakeness,
When I know that I need to live my life with
faith.
I don't want to act out my life for attention,
But to live my life in desperation–
Not for the one who hurt me,
But for the One who hurt Himself for me.

All my fake dramas
And my fake smiles,
My fake agony
And groanings–
I wish all would end.

My mad thoughts and ill friend
Will someday come to an end,
With laughter and smiles only left.

God can understand you well,
More than your actions and sayings well said.
Let not my life be filled with fakeness,
Rather, let there be light
To change me completely and fill me with
gladness.

More than Hope

Your lost hope will be renewed,
So deep and vast – beyond what's viewed.
More than your expectations wild,
Never too low, nor meek, nor mild.

But time has a purpose for hope to grow,
And nature will wait if God wills it so.
Beyond imagination, your dreams will arise,
With joy complete and spirits revived.

No more tears and sorrow untold,
For they will pass and soon grow old.
Hope stays true, so firm and bright,
When placed in God, it's guiding light.

With faith, not doubt, deep inside,
Your hope in Him will not subside.
It will never fade nor be cast off,
But rise in glory – placed on top!

Leave Your Stained Garment

Leave it to the One who made it stained,
Yes, the garments of sin and suffering.
Leave it to the one who destroyed your dreams,
For with him, you have no part or means.

The enemy of your soul – you know it,
You no longer need that garment unfit.
God wants to clothe you with a branded firmament,
A robe of grace, pure and permanent.

Wear it every day without delay,
It will change you in every way.
Never let the enemy steal your new one,
A gift of love from God's own Son.

Never think of the old stained garment,
For what was given is new and marvellous.
Enjoy each moment, walk in light,
It fills your soul with strength and might.

The garment of hope and salvation divine,
A gift from God – forever thine.

My Tears

Consider my tears as balm at Your feet,
Pouring out jars completely broken,
With hearts deeply open,

Not wasting even a single drop–
Not on any man or mortal loss.

I find pleasure in doing it so,
Never bothering with how costly it was made
and sold.

I know to whom I pour,
Its worth will be measured – or not, I do not
know.
But my Saviour will know,
How my heart is crushed and deeply torn.

He considered it, now bent down and behold,
He touched me and my broken jar.
He said, 'You have not wasted it, and you will
no more.
Go back, for I have granted what you have
asked for.
I have considered your tears as balm at My
feet!'

Not Forgotten

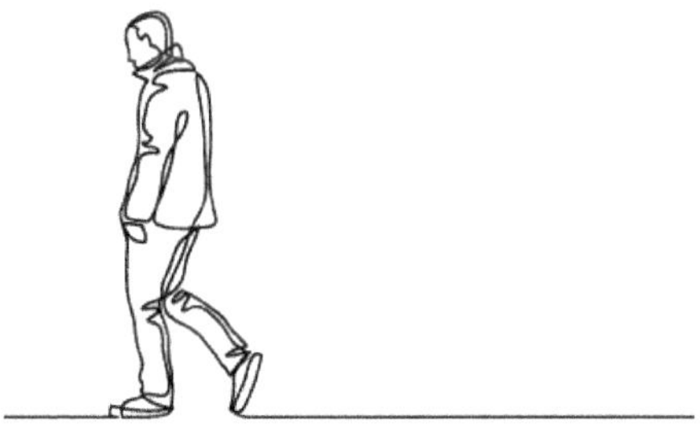

You are not forgotten,
Neither are the promises rotten.
They are alive, ready to bring life,
When your strength wanes, remember these
promises; they will make you smile.

It all takes time,
It doesn't mean God has forgotten your cries.
He takes time, and He knows that your heart
pains.
He knows when to act – His ways are wise.

He is the Master of all, in fact,
Never failing, never slack.
Never doubt His promises so true,
He has not forgotten or given up on you.

Your dreams and longingness remain,
In His time, they won't be in vain.
God has woven you so beautifully,
You are His own, made with dignity.

How can He forget or leave you to suffer,
His own dear child to wander and to be
considered as litter?
You are not forgotten,
Not forgotten by the One who has begotten!

Wilderness

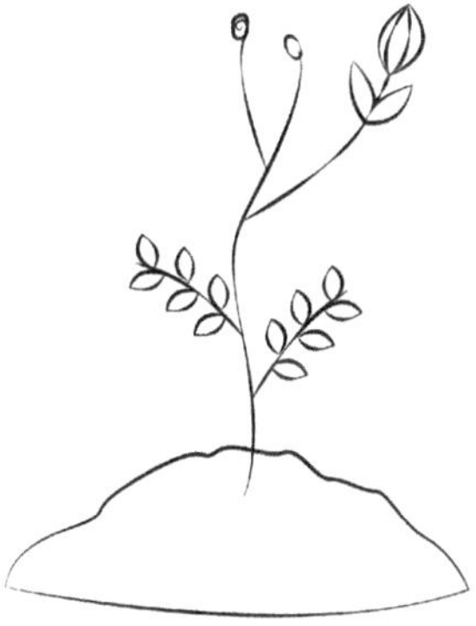

God knows you are going through this great
wilderness,
Walking and walking, tired of struggles and
homelessness,
Weary of expecting good things
And failing to acknowledge the presence of
His powerful deeds.

God says He has seen your struggle,
But be still – He will fight for you, so do not
rebel.
He has kept a great land for you,
And He will strengthen you to reach it with
renewed energy.

He knows the great wilderness you are
walking through,
And He will not leave you forsaken – this is
true.
The wilderness will turn into a blessing
When you trust God – that will be a sure
thing.

Be not dismayed, for He is with you in this
journey,
And you will testify that He was true,

That it was a beautiful symphony.

Sorrow and Love

Sorrow met love on the cross,
For you and me to be free.
The nail-pierced hands and legs
For us to walk in love and be in bliss,
Not to sin anymore and think of it no more.

His head was crowned with thorns,
For it was sorrowful and sour,
But it was for us to be pure.

It was all for His love's sake, He endured,
Not compelled but willingly taken,
For us to live a life truthful and not shaken.

To be different from the world,
And to take up our own cross,
And walk to become like Him, who finished
His task.

For you and me, He met sorrow on that cross,
To produce love, set us free and not be lost.

Power of Weeping

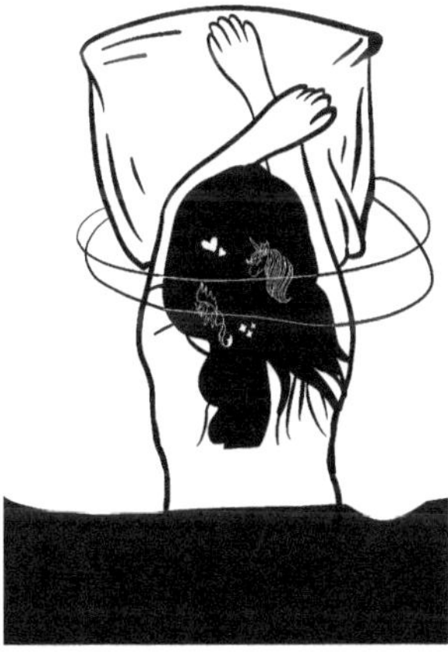

When you feel that your weeping has no end,
It means there's a greater hope and a grand
new beginning ahead.
It holds more power than any speech or
mighty note,
For they may never know its worth, though it
grows and overflows.

You may cry through the day and night,
Not knowing why these tears fall all the time.
At times, the reasons may remain unknown,
Yet they leave you broken and alone.

Your weeping may seem unending,
But remember, God has set a time and a
boundary.
Even sorrow cannot take control over you,
Until God commands it to stop and go no
further.

Your weeping carries a greater purpose,
For God knows why you weep – it is vast and
weighty.
He sees you, He hears you and He knows your
pain,
And through your tears, a deep fountain of
blessings is being made.

Your weeping will surely cease,
And you will witness the sunlight's release.
A beautiful light will shine upon you once
more,
Bringing an end to sorrow – your weeping
had a purpose, and it will be no more.

Never to Shame

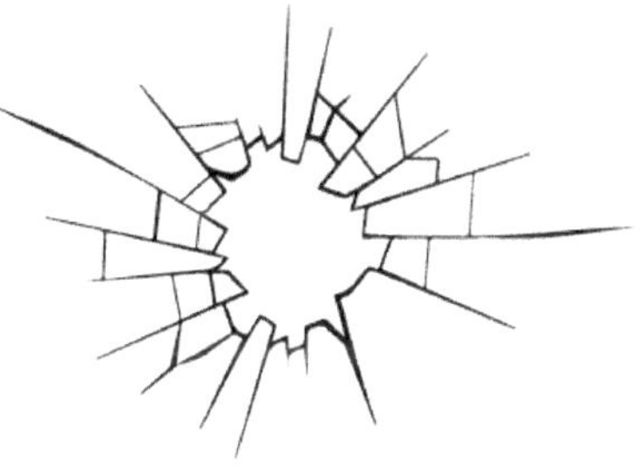

God will never put you to shame
Before others or leave your life in blame.
Remember, you have trusted Him,
And He will never let your faith grow dim.

You might be kind to them,
Humble and meek before them,
But it's not your fault if they look down on
you
Or think you are their equal, easy to subdue.

Since you trust God, you are never just
anyone–
You are special, set apart, second to none.
The world may call it grandeur,
But you are God's design, perfect and dear.

Trust Him, and He will lift you high.
Walk by faith; let sight pass by.
Never in shame – never will it be–
For those who trust and walk faithfully.

Perfect Peace

When you trust God, you'll have peace–
Perfect peace in abundance, and you will find
ease.
Your heart will not fear or waver,
Nor be in terror like a nightmare dreamer.

When you trust God, like the foundation of
stone,
Your faith will never be shaken, even when
the earth groans.
You will be called blessed
When you trust in God and see His
abundance.

Lean on Him firmly,
So that you may receive His blessings timely.
Peace is guaranteed swiftly
When you learn to trust in God hourly.

It's not just peace – it's perfect peace indeed,
Never lacking for those who trust God in
every need.

Offering

Offer yourself as a burnt offering
All the bad deeds and qualities
To God as a sacrifice
For you to become Holy and nice

Never neglect your lonely hours
For it is good and precious for your
transformation

Offer everything you have
For God can change you completely and more
Your heart and mind will be renewed and
tuned
According to His will and in one accordance
when you are pruned

Leave everything and surrender to Him
For He can shape and mould you for Him
Burn every jealousy and anger
They may not need you any longer

Not Defeated

You are not defeated,
Never cast down nor mistreated.
You are born to win–
The battle with the sin.

You will not be defeated,
But born to conquer, highly seated.
The enemy cannot frighten you;
Instead, he will flee from view.

No matter if the king of Og comes near,
Nor his mighty iron bed brings fear.
You will surely overcome the mighty,
With the help of God's sovereignty.

You will not be shaken nor moved,
For victory is certain and proved.
You are not defeated,
But born to live free and uncheated.

You can fight against any giants–
Be it Nephilim, Goliath or lions.
You are born to conquer,
And never to be defeated!

Silent Cries

God knows your heart's desires;
He will fulfil them in great ways for you
to aspire!

He has listened to your
unspoken words.
He knows you did not have
the courage to letter those words.

He has heard your prayers
the silent ones,
which no one knows
Because they are secret.

He has seen your cries,
the hurting heart and aching eyes,
the groanings of your heart.

He has taken them into account.
Your anxious thoughts
He's ready to respond.

The silent cry, He has noticed it.
Since you are His beloved,
He has not neglected it.

Press On

When you are in distress,
When hard times come and disturb.
Lean on God, for it will be well.

You will not be moved,
You will not be broken.

Keep pressing on,
Move forward with the Lord.

Lift up your voice unto God,
He will deliver you,
He will answer your call.

Just press on,
Just hold on.

You will surely see
A beautiful sea,
Without blemish or grease!

Just press on!

Battle!

The battle you face may be strong,
The battle you face may be wild.
It can take you under and over,
Beating your heart faster.
It can pull you down and make you weaker–
All because you don't use the right weapon
To fight against the evil planner.

Remember to put on the armour,
The one that is true.
It holds the power to fight
Against the unknown enemy–
Bold, scary and full of irony.

You can win this fight
When you learn God's will.
Be strong and bold,
For the Word in you
Will wage war against the enemy as a whole.

Resist

I know it's hard for you to resist,
Not one or two, but plenty persist.
Within yourself, you're burdened tight,
Leave it to God; don't start a fight.

Don't say the words you long to speak,
Don't let your anger reach its peak.
Don't show the things you wish to reveal,
Let God alone your heart unseal.

Jealous eyes will rage and stare,
But only God is just and fair.
Even the closest may betray,
They too will fail; they too will stray.

Real Change!

Your day will come,
only when your strength wanes,
And in God, when your strength relied,
The expected change will come,
When your knees hit the ground and
surrender becomes your only hope!

Hope will rise like an eagle till the sun,
Not wavering, weak nor falling down,
Cast heavy, or eyes sunken and drowned.

Try not to change you,
Exchange with the One who gave Himself to
you.

He does things best,
By changing your worst,
To fly high and not slow down,
Soaring higher, never to drown.

Desired change will come
When God's strength replaces yours,
And you will see new ways and opened doors.

A City not Forsaken

You will be called as a city
A city not forsaken
Your land will not be desolate
And not barren

God has built your walls
You will rise again and war
The victory is yours
On this, be sure
He has not left you

He will never stay quiet and untrue
He will establish your feet
And make you a diadem and His bride
You are a city not forsaken
For the Lord is with you, and you will not be
shaken!

Be Confident

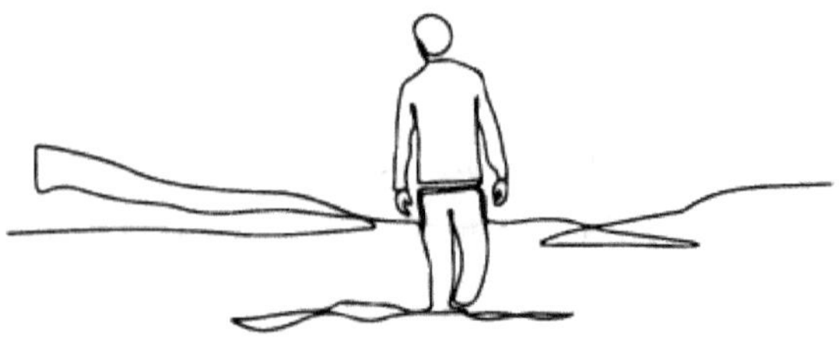

The Lord who began a good work in you
Will surely complete it, faithful and true.
No delay, no pause, no turn away,
His promises stand – He'll never stray.

Trust in Him with all your heart,
For He is faithful, set apart.
Disappointment will not be your end,
Your cries reach Him – your dearest friend.

Your righteousness will brightly shine,
A testament to His love divine.
Blessings will come in endless measure,
And sorrow will turn into a stored treasure.

One day, your tears will tell the story
Of unwavering trust and God's great glory.

Midst of Fire

Never regret for walking through fire
For God's word will be heard in your need
There will be joy when you hear
His sweet voice and when He is near
It is painful when you walk on fire
But you will not be consumed for God is with
you; do not fear
The experience will be hard
But the outcome will be beautiful and not
drought
For you will hear God's voice
Which is so tender and nice
What else you need?
More than hearing the one who made you and
me
The universe and the sea
Midst of fire!

Quieten Your Soul

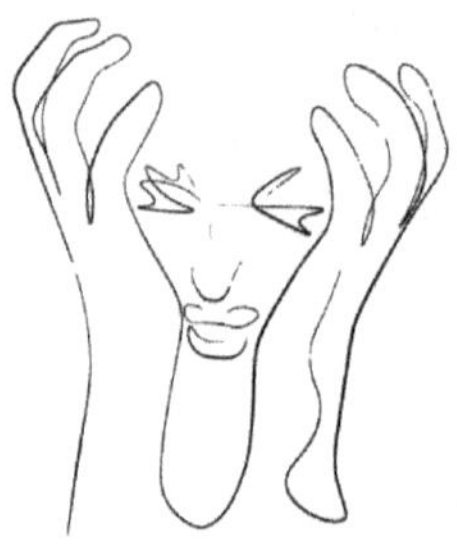

With God's love, your restless heart will find
peace,
Your lonely soul will be mended with ease.
He will rejoice over you with singing,
For His love is deep and unending.

The Lord is near – He dwells within,
A mighty warrior who saves and defends.
He will fight your battles, stand by your side,
In His strength, you can safely abide.

So trust in Him – do not be afraid,
For He is your salvation, your anchor, your
aid.
He delights in you and makes all things good,
Calming your spirit, restoring your mood.

He Will Calm Your Fears

When fear is raging high,
Leave it to God – don't be shy.
He longs to calm your trembling soul,
To bring you peace, to make you whole.

Do you wonder how He'll do it?
Trust and wait – that's the secret to it.

Breathe in, breathe out,
Let go of your anxious doubts.
Place your worries in a basket,
Lift them up – He'll surpass it.

Let your broken heart be healed,
Give Him the pain you've concealed.
Your mind is drowning in restless waves,
You're fighting hard – desperate to escape.
You wish for silence, for thoughts to fade,
Even an empty void would feel like grace.

But do you remember what I said?
God will calm your fears, not just mend.
He'll wrap you in His endless love,
A love so real – so strong enough.

No One!

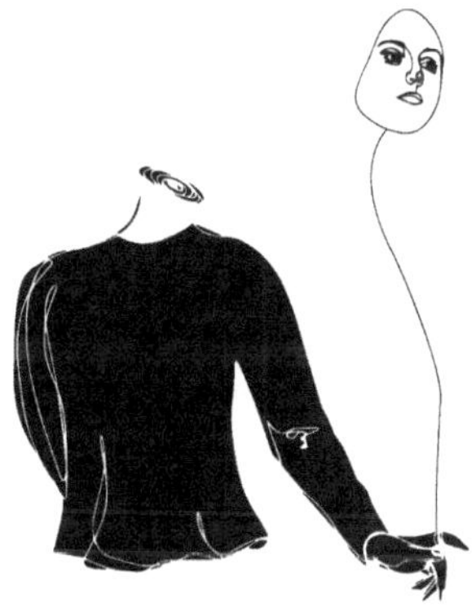

When you wait for God with patience,
You will see His glory in excellence.
No eye has seen what He has in store,
No ear has heard His wonders before.

Everything happens in His perfect time,
Wait in patience – you'll see His blessings
align.

But He will not stay quiet for sure,
Because you think of Him more and more.
He won't just come when you are in need,
For He dwells within you – in every deed.

No one can see what He has planned,
So they cannot judge or understand.
Let them mock your trials today,
For soon, His truth will light the way.

A time will come – things will be revealed,
They will see their doubts repealed.
They will know they were wrong indeed,
And humbly heed to God's great lead.

Until then, no one will ever know
What God has written for you to show.
No matter how hard they try to see,
His masterpiece remains a mystery.

His grand design He keeps secure,
But one day soon, it will be sure–
With awe and wonder, all will see,
And raise their brows in disbelief!

Expectations

Let your expectations come from God,
For they'll be great, and you'll not be flawed.
He is present every moment in time,
So you won't cry in despair or pine.

He will never disappoint you,
In His perfect plan, you'll see what's true.
He is God and not mere man,
Righteous and good – His love will stand.

He will fulfil all your desires,
Like a bride awaiting love that never tires.
Let your expectations rest in the Lord,
Your heart will be filled and not ignored.

No Turning Back

Obey God, lest you be chastised,
Follow His statutes and be revived.
He warned Solomon to do the same,
And calls you now in a voice untamed.

Never turn your back on God,
Lest His guiding hand withdraw.
Follow and love Him true,
So His forgiveness may rest on you.

Let Him not cast you from His sight,
But in His word, take deep delight.

Humble yourself, seek and pray,
And He will bless with grace each day.

All Things Well

God makes all things well,
Bringing beauty to bloom, where goodness
dwells.
Miracles flow to hearts that yield,
Surrendered fully to His will revealed.

He is able to set things right,
Turning fear and darkness into light.
He makes all things well,
Leading you to pastures green and wells that
swell.

Your loneliness – He makes it bright,
Filling it with songs and joy in sight.

All things will work together still,
For those who love Him and trust His will.

Come What May!

Life can bring many storms
Many trials and with lessons along
Be not dismayed looking at it
Let your heart trust Him who allowed it

Your emotions cannot handle it
Your anger can have no control over it
Leave it to God lest you get wearied and torn

Hard days, unexpected waves can hit you
some days
Hold on tight for God has greater heights
You will cross this sea, treading and fearful
With sustained ease with God's strength and
peace.

Come what may!

Decisions

Vivid dreams, confusing voices,
Scared to take bold choices.
Leaving opportunities unchecked,
Living a life filled with regret.

Is this all I'm meant to face,
As I think about my fate?
What's my next phase,
When everyone seems to be in their right
place?

Yet, I still have hope inside,
Even when my tears have dried.
That hope is in God alone,
Who restores with laughter, not sorrow's
tone.

Your hope will never be cut off,
When your decisions are in His hands, held
aloft!

Vulnerable

You may be sick – sick of words,
Hurting, fearful, weary, unheard.
You may be vulnerable to disappointments,
Growing cold with weakened endurance.

You may not be strong to bear what's wrong,
Yes, you may feel vulnerable all along.

But take it now as an opportunity,
To turn it for good, for strength, for beauty.
Heed your heart to the voice of God,
Not to hurtful thoughts or words that prod.

Your vulnerability will fade away,
Your testimony will shine one day.

You will be called vulnerable no more,
Your fears will vanish; you'll be restored.
No longer accused, nor held to blame,
But free to rise, unshaken again.

Live Free

You are no longer bound by harsh words,
By tones that crush and leave you hurt.

No more chained by loneliness or fear,
Freed at last from torment near.
No more accused of thoughts untrue,
Relieved of burdens that once subdued.

You are set free by God's embrace,
To live with joy, unchained by fate.

No longer imprisoned by intimidation,
Nor trapped by doubt or hesitation.
But freed to choose – not evil nor strife,
But a path of joy, a fulfilled life.

Going in Silence

When anger rages
And fear daunts you day and night
When mood swings and makes your emotions
flight
When you lose control and cannot hold your
temper tight
Go in silence, go in peace
Let that be your defence for you to experience
peace

Vengeance is not yours
Nor the anger to blame someone
Leave it to God and go in silence

Be still and let God take your emotions
Speak not a word; neither hurt your heart so
hard

Let your feelings move in the air
For the one who watches your feelings knows
it well

Go in silence!

Fear Not, Fret Not

Is tomorrow's worry keeping you awake?
Is fear of the future too much to take?

Does shivering seize and shake your soul?
Do your words turn to tears that silently roll?

Thinking too deep of what lies ahead,
Does your heart tremble, filled with dread?
But tomorrow is not yours to hold,
Fret not – it's secured, as foretold.

Leave it to God – He knows what's best,
In His hands, your soul finds rest.

Fear not,
Fret not,
Leave it to God, and worry not!

Thirsty

You thirst so much, weak and drained,
Scared your life may wither in pain.
Basic needs remain unmet,
Deepest longings filled with unrest.

Not wanting to be a burden or unwell,
You say it's not okay for you or them.
Your soul longs for love and affirmation,
Yet they failed you with empty declarations.

They promised to give in double measure,
But left you with tears and nothing to
treasure.
You wasted your life trusting those words,
Only to find they were never yours.

Do you long for living waters?
To refresh your weary soul?
To replenish, renew and make you whole?

Leave behind the ones who deceived,
Understand, their words were make-believe.

Living waters can satisfy more,
Until you say, 'It's marvellous!
I wish I had known before'.

Forgiveness

The hardest phrase I have ever known–
To let go of heartaches and harsh words,
To forgive and not remember anymore,
To release the heartbreaks and deep wounds.

Feelings of being useless, of being used,
The faults too heavy to bear or excuse,
The lies that ache and echo in ears,
Time and again, even after years.

Yes, it's hard – your heart resists,
Wounded by wrongs it can't dismiss.
Anger bursting through your veins,
With no escape, no way to explain.

But think – does God not feel the same?
Does His anger not rise, yet still remain
A love so vast, a grace so true?
Didn't He let go and forgive you?

Did your heart not rejoice, amazed,
At the mercy and love He gave?
Then let it go, give another chance,
For God has given you more than one glance.

Go, forgive!